ADVANTAGE

Pupil's Edition

Georgia Test Preparation

CRCT and Stanford 9

Includes Test Taking Tips and
math assessment items for
- multiple choice format
- short answer
- extended response

Grade 1

Harcourt Brace & Company

Orlando • Atlanta • Austin • Boston • San Francisco • Chicago • Dallas • New York • Toronto • London
http://www.hbschool.com

ISBN 0-15-321593-3

2 3 4 5 6 7 8 9 10 073 2003 2002 2001

CONTENTS

TEST 1 Chapters 1-2
Addition and Subtraction
Concepts 1

TEST 2 Chapters 3-6
Addition and Subtraction
Facts to 10 7

TEST 3 Chapters 7-10
Geometry, Spatial Sense,
and Patterns 13

TEST 4 Chapters 11-12
Addition and Subtraction
Facts to 12 19

TEST 5 Chapters 13-15
Place Value and Numbers
Patterns 25

TEST 6 Chapters 16-19
Money and Time 31

TEST 7 Chapters 20-22
Measurement and Fractions 37

TEST 8 Chapters 23-24
Working with Data 43

TEST 9 Chapters 25-26
Addition and Subtraction
Facts to 18 49

TEST 10 Chapters 27-28
Exploring Multiplication, Division,
and Two-Digit Addition and
Subtraction 55

v

© Harcourt

Math Advantage Georgia Test Prep   **Grade 1**

Choose the correct answer.

1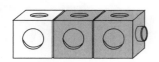

1 + 2 = _____

- (A) 3
- (B) 4
- (C) 5
- (D) NOT HERE

2

3 frogs jump.
1 frog sits.
How many in all?

- (F) 2 frogs
- (H) 4 frogs
- (G) 3 frogs
- (J) 5 frogs

3

4 + 1 = _____

- (A) 3
- (C) 5
- (B) 4
- (D) NOT HERE

4

4 + 2 = _____

- (F) 3
- (H) 5
- (G) 4
- (J) NOT HERE

5 Which addition sentence tells how many in all?

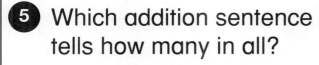

- (A) 2 + 1 = 3
- (B) 3 + 1 = 4
- (C) 4 + 1 = 5
- (D) 5 + 1 = 6

6 Which addition sentence tells how many in all?

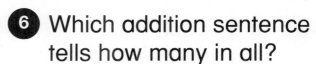

- (F) 4 + 2 = 6
- (G) 3 + 2 = 5
- (H) 2 + 2 = 4
- (J) 1 + 2 = 3

GO ON

7

4 pups play.
I walks away.
How many are left?

(A) I pup   (C) 3 pups
(B) 2 pups   (D) 4 pups

8

6 birds eat.
3 fly away.
How many are left?

(F) 2 birds   (H) 4 birds
(G) 3 birds   (J) 6 birds

9 Which subtraction sentence shows how many are left?

(A) 6 − 3 = 3   (C) 5 − I = 4
(B) 5 − 2 = 3   (D) 4 − 0 = 4

10 Which subtraction sentence shows how many are left?

(F) 6 − I = 5   (H) 6 − 3 = 3
(G) 6 − 2 = 4   (J) 6 − 4 = 2

11 Add or subtract.
Use counters.

2 fish swim.
2 more come.
How many in all?

(A) 2 fish   (C) 4 fish
(B) 3 fish   (D) 5 fish

12 Add or subtract.
Use counters.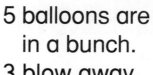

5 balloons are
in a bunch.
3 blow away.
How many are left?

(F) 2 balloons   (H) 4 balloons
(G) 3 balloons   (J) 5 balloons

Name _____

13 Draw 1 more.

Write the sum.

3 + 1 = ___

....

14 How many in all?

Write the sum.

4 + 2 = ___

....

15 My domino has 2 dots on each side. How many dots in all?

Draw the story. Write the addition sentence.

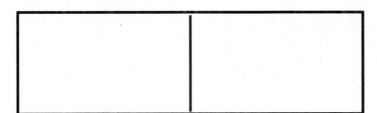

___ + ___ = ___

© Harcourt

16 Cross out 1.

Write how many are left.

4 − 1 = ___

17 Cross out 2.

Write the difference.

6 − 2 = ___

18 Write the subtraction sentence.

  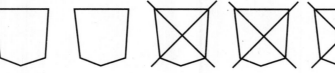

___ − ___ = ___

GO ON

Name _____

19 Write the difference.

◯ ◯ ◯ ◯ ⊗

| 5 | | − | | 1 | | = | | |

······································

20 Add or subtract.

Use counters.

Draw the counters.

6 trucks park.

1 truck goes.

How many trucks are left?

_____ trucks

STOP

© Harcourt

Choose the correct answer.

1

$4 + 5 = $ _____

Ⓐ 6   Ⓒ 8
Ⓑ 7   Ⓓ 9

2 Find the missing sum.

$3 + 2 = 5$

$2 + 3 = $ _____

Ⓕ 5   Ⓗ 7
Ⓖ 6   Ⓙ 8

3 Use counters.

Which is a way to make 8?

Ⓐ $2 + 4$ Ⓒ $5 + 2$
Ⓑ $5 + 3$ Ⓓ $7 + 2$

4 Count on to add.

$8 + 1 = $ _____

Ⓕ 6   Ⓗ 9
Ⓖ 8   Ⓙ 10

5

Kim has 6 berries.
Mom gives her 3 more.
How many berries
does Kim have now?

Ⓐ 3   Ⓒ 9
Ⓑ 6   Ⓓ 10

6 Find the doubles fact that goes with the picture.

Ⓕ $2 + 2 = 4$
Ⓖ $3 + 3 = 6$
Ⓗ $4 + 4 = 8$
Ⓙ NOT HERE

© Harcourt

7

6 frogs are on a log.
2 jump off.
How many frogs now?

(A) 2 frogs   (C) 4 frogs
(B) 3 frogs   (D) NOT HERE

8 $6 + 3 = 9$
$3 + 6 = 9$
$9 - 3 = 6$
$9 - 6 = $ _____

(F) 2   (H) 4
(G) 3   (J) 5

9

$$\begin{array}{r} 5 \\ +0 \\ \hline \end{array}$$

(A) 5   (C) 7
(B) 6   (D) 8

10

$$\begin{array}{r} 4 \\ -0 \\ \hline \end{array}$$

(F) 0   (H) 3
(G) 2   (J) 4

11

$9 - 3 = $ _____

(A) 5   (C) 7
(B) 6   (D) 8

12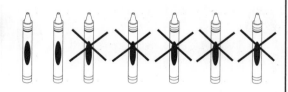

$$\begin{array}{r} 7 \\ -5 \\ \hline \end{array}$$

(F) 0   (H) 2
(G) 1   (J) 3

GO ON

13 Color  to show one way to make 7.
Write the number sentence.

○ ○ ○ ○ ○ ○ ○

____ + ____ = ____

14 Toss 10 two-color counters.

Write how many red and how many yellow
for each toss.

How many different ways can you make 10?

15 Write the sums. Circle the one with doubles.

$$\begin{array}{r} 5 \\ + 5 \\ \hline \end{array}$$

$$\begin{array}{r} 4 \\ + 3 \\ \hline \end{array}$$

GO ON

16 Draw a picture to solve.

6 blue flowers grow.

3 red flowers grow.

How many flowers grow in all? _____ flowers

....

17 Use counters.
Solve.

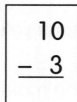

....

18 Use 10 counters. Show a fact family.

Draw a picture.

Write two number sentences.

____ + ____ = ____

____ + ____ = ____

GO ON

19 Use the number line.
Count back to subtract.

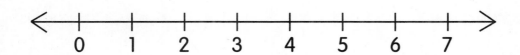

$$7 - 3 = \underline{}$$

20

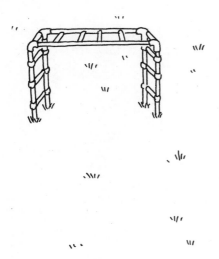

Draw to solve.

Ashley is at the park.

Six girls come.

How many girls are there in all?   _____ girls

Did you use addition or subtraction? _____

STOP

Name _____

Choose the correct answer.

1 What is the name of this plane figure?

Ⓐ rectangle Ⓒ square
Ⓑ circle Ⓓ triangle

2 What is the name of this solid figure?

Ⓕ sphere Ⓗ cube
Ⓖ cone Ⓙ NOT HERE

3 Which figure has 4 sides and 4 corners?

Ⓐ △ Ⓒ □

Ⓑ ⬠ Ⓓ ○

4 Which plane figure has the same shape?

Ⓕ □ Ⓗ ▭

Ⓖ ○ Ⓙ △

5 Which shape is **larger than** this one?

Ⓐ ○ Ⓑ ◯

6 Which shape is the **same size as** this one?

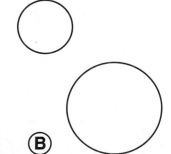

Ⓕ ▭ Ⓖ ▭

Name _____

Use the grid for questions
7 and 8.

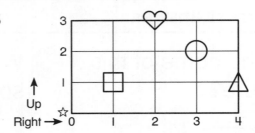

---

7 Start at ☆. Go right 3.
Go up 2. Which shape
is there?

Ⓐ ◯   Ⓒ △

Ⓑ ♡   Ⓓ ☐

8 Start at ☆. Go right 4.
Go up 1. Which shape
is there?

Ⓕ ◯   Ⓗ △

Ⓖ ♡   Ⓙ ☐

---

9 Which line makes two
sides that match?

Ⓐ

Ⓒ

Ⓑ

Ⓓ

10 Which picture shows the
bird **inside** the cage?

Ⓕ

Ⓖ

---

11 Which is next in the
pattern?

Ⓐ   Ⓒ

Ⓑ   Ⓓ

12 What number is next in
the pattern?

2, 4, 6, 8, 10, ___

Ⓕ 8   Ⓗ 12
Ⓖ 10   Ⓙ 14

Math Advantage Georgia Test Prep   14   GO ON ➤

© Harcourt

13 Circle the ones you can stack.

....

14 Circle the shapes with a round face.

....

15 What shape could you trace from each?
Draw each shape below.

<u>Idea Bank</u>

square

triangle

rectangle

Name _____

16 Make a figure the same size and shape.

....

17 Draw a line of symmetry on each of these pictures.

© Harcourt

18 Draw the other side of the picture.
Talk about what you did.

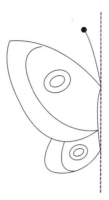

....

19 Use connecting cubes of 2 colors. Make a pattern.
Tell how your pattern repeats.

....

20 Tell how this pattern repeats. _____

Use these same objects to draw a new pattern.
Repeat 2 times.

STOP

Name _____

Choose the correct answer.

1

$6 + 4 = $ _____

Ⓐ 9   Ⓒ 12

Ⓑ 11   Ⓓ NOT HERE

2

$$\begin{array}{r} 4 \\ +4 \\ \hline \end{array}$$

Ⓕ 6   Ⓗ 8

Ⓖ 7   Ⓙ NOT HERE

3

$$\begin{array}{r} 3 \\ 5 \\ +2 \\ \hline \end{array}$$

Ⓐ 9   Ⓒ 12

Ⓑ 10   Ⓓ NOT HERE

4

$$\begin{array}{r} 9 \\ 2 \\ +1 \\ \hline \end{array}$$

Ⓕ 10   Ⓗ 12

Ⓖ 11   Ⓙ NOT HERE

5 Ben spent 7¢.
Jan spent 5¢.
How much did they
spend in all?

Ⓐ 10¢   Ⓒ 12¢

Ⓑ 11¢   Ⓓ 13¢

6 5 birds are eating.
6 more birds come to eat.
How many birds are
eating?

Ⓕ 11 birds   Ⓗ 13 birds

Ⓖ 12 birds   Ⓙ 14 birds

7 How many more fish than turtles are there?

$$\begin{array}{r} 10 \\ -\ 7 \\ \hline \end{array}$$

Ⓐ 2   Ⓒ 4
Ⓑ 3   Ⓓ 5

8 Which number sentence belongs in this fact family?

$11 - 4 = 7$
$11 - 7 = 4$
$7 + 4 = 11$

Ⓕ $4 + 3 = 7$
Ⓖ $4 + 7 = 11$
Ⓗ $11 - 6 = 5$
Ⓙ $7 - 4 = 3$

9
$$\begin{array}{r} 7 \\ +2 \\ \hline 9 \end{array} \qquad \begin{array}{r} 9 \\ -2 \\ \hline \end{array}$$

Ⓐ 6   Ⓒ 8
Ⓑ 7   Ⓓ NOT HERE

10

```
 ←—+——+——+——+——+——+——+——+——→
   5   6   7   8   9  10  11  12
```

$11 - 5 = \underline{\quad}$

Ⓕ 4   Ⓗ 6
Ⓖ 5   Ⓙ NOT HERE

11 Which number sentence does the story show?

Carlos had 12 apples.
He gave away 5.
How many are left?

Ⓐ $12 - 5 = 7$
Ⓑ $2 + 3 = 5$
Ⓒ $12 - 7 = 5$
Ⓓ NOT HERE

12 Which number sentence does the story show?

Ana had 4 fish.
She got 8 more.
How many does she have?

Ⓕ $12 - 4 = 8$
Ⓖ $4 + 4 = 8$
Ⓗ $12 - 8 = 4$
Ⓙ $4 + 8 = 12$

13 Show how to make a sum of 12 in 4 different ways.

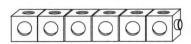 

____+____= ____   ____+____= ____

____+____= ____   ____+____= ____

....

14 Use cubes to find 3 numbers that add to 11.
Draw a picture.

Write the number sentence.

____+____+____= 11

....

15 Tell an addition story.
Write the number sentence.
Solve.

7 books

5 books

____+____= ____

16 Read the story. Draw a picture to solve it.

Nine students each need a pencil.

There are 5 pencils.

How many more pencils are needed?

_____ pencils

· ·

17 Use these cubes.

Write the sum.

$$8 \quad + \quad 3 \quad = \_\_\_$$

Write three more facts from this family.

___+___= ___   ___+___= ___

___+___= ___

· ·

18 Write the missing number.
Use cubes in the ten frame to help.

$$12 - \boxed{} = 7$$

GO ON

19 Write the number sentence for the story.

A pet store has 11 dogs and 6 cats.

How many more dogs than cats are there?

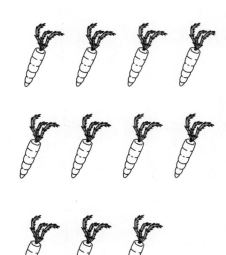

____ ◯ ____ = ____

···

20 Solve. Write the number sentence.

Ann grew 11 carrots.

Brandon grew 7 carrots.

How many more carrots did Ann grow?

____ ◯ ____ = ____

STOP

Choose the correct answer.

1 How many?

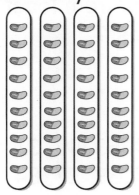

(A) 3 ones = 3
(B) 3 tens = 30
(C) 4 tens = 40
(D) 5 tens = 50

2 How many?

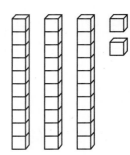

(F) 1 ten + 3 ones = 13
(G) 3 tens + 2 ones = 32
(H) 3 tens + 3 ones = 33
(J) NOT HERE

3 How many?

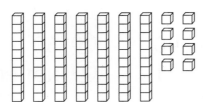

(A) 78   (C) 87
(B) 80   (D) NOT HERE

4 Jan picked a number **between** 55 and 57. Which number did she pick?

(F) 54   (H) 58
(G) 56   (J) 60

5 Which number comes just **before** 97?

_____, 97

(A) 79   (C) 90
(B) 87   (D) 96

6 Which is the better estimate?

(F) more than ten
(G) fewer than ten

7 Which number is **greater**?

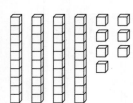

Ⓐ 47   Ⓑ 34

8 Which numbers are in order from **least** to **greatest**?

Ⓕ 64, 53, 42, 31
Ⓖ 15, 39, 27, 84
Ⓗ 32, 46, 57, 66

9 Count by twos. Which number comes **after** 14?

Ⓐ 12   Ⓒ 15
Ⓑ 13   Ⓓ 16

10 Count by tens. Which number comes **after** 50?

Ⓕ 40   Ⓗ 60
Ⓖ 51   Ⓙ NOT HERE

11 Count by fives. Which number comes **after** 35?

Ⓐ 30   Ⓒ 40
Ⓑ 36   Ⓓ 45

12 Even or odd?

11

Ⓕ even   Ⓖ odd

GO ON

© Harcourt

13 These two pictures show 30.

What is another way to show 30?

Draw it here.

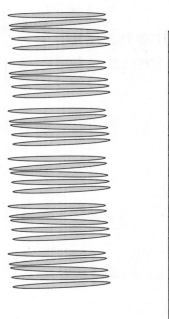
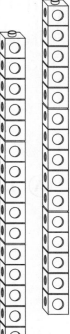

....

14 How many crackers on each tray?

_____   _____

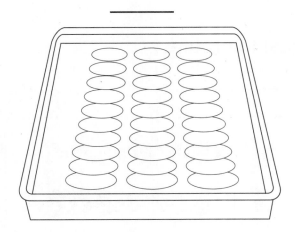
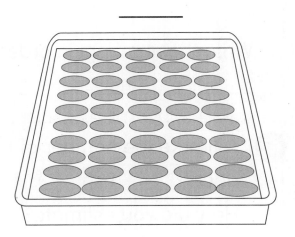

Circle the tray that has more.

Draw a line under the tray that has fewer.

15 Write the numbers.
Circle the number that is the greatest.

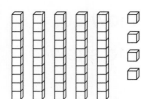

_____

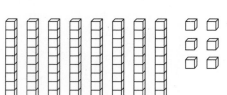

_____

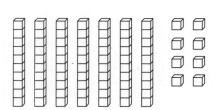

_____

16 Use cubes or base-ten blocks to show each number.

54   24   74   48

Write the numbers in order from least to greatest.

_____   _____   _____   _____

17 Estimate the number of fish.
about _____ fish
How did you estimate?

_____

_____

_____

GO ON

18 Write the missing numbers.

1	2	3	4		6	7	8	9	
11	12	13	14		16	17	18	19	
21	22	23	24		26	27	28	29	
31	32	33	34		36	37	38	39	

Talk about the patterns you see.

19 Color squares to show 12.

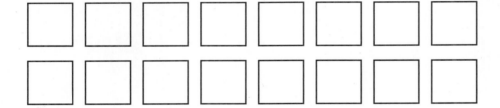

Circle even or odd.   even   odd

Tell how you know.

20 Draw a model to show that 7 is an odd number.

Tell about it.

STOP

Name _____

Choose the correct answer.

1 What is the value of this coin?

Ⓐ 1¢   Ⓒ 5¢
Ⓑ 2¢   Ⓓ 10¢

2 What is the name of this coin?

Ⓕ penny   Ⓗ quarter
Ⓖ nickel   Ⓙ dime

3 Which amount do these coins add up to?

Ⓐ 8¢   Ⓒ 14¢
Ⓑ 10¢   Ⓓ NOT HERE

4 Which amount do these coins add up to?

Ⓕ 4¢   Ⓗ 21¢
Ⓖ 16¢   Ⓙ 26¢

5 Which coins have the same value as ?

Ⓐ 1 dime, 1 nickel
Ⓑ 2 dimes, 1 nickel
Ⓒ 2 dimes, 2 pennies
Ⓓ 3 dimes, 5 pennies

6 Which toy can you buy with

    ?

Ⓕ  37¢

Ⓖ 28¢

Ⓗ 32¢

Ⓙ 41¢

© Harcourt

GO ON ➡

Name _____

Use the calendar to answer questions 7, 8, and 9.

December

S	M	T	W	T	F	S
				1	2	3
4	5	6	7	8	9	10
11	12	13	14	15	16	17
18	19	20	21	22	23	24
25	26	27	28	29	30	31

---

7 On which day is December 17?

Ⓐ Friday   Ⓒ Sunday
Ⓑ Saturday Ⓓ Monday

8 How many days are there in 1 week?

Ⓕ 3 days   Ⓗ 6 days
Ⓖ 5 days   Ⓙ 7 days

---

9 What is the date of the last Tuesday?

Ⓐ December 20
Ⓑ December 27
Ⓒ December 28
Ⓓ December 30

10 About how long does it take to do this?

Ⓕ a minute   Ⓗ a week
Ⓖ an hour   Ⓙ a month

---

11 Which clock shows the same time?

Ⓐ 1:00   Ⓒ 3:00
Ⓑ  2:00   Ⓓ NOT HERE

12 What time is it?

Ⓕ 9:30   Ⓗ 10:30
Ⓖ 10:00   Ⓙ NOT HERE

Math Advantage Georgia Test Prep   32

13 Use pennies or cubes to model.

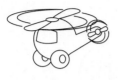

5¢

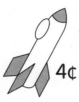

4¢

Draw how many pennies.

Write the total amount.

_____ ¢ + _____ ¢ = _____ ¢

· ·

14 You have 6¢.

What can you buy?

Draw your answer.

Write the number
sentence.

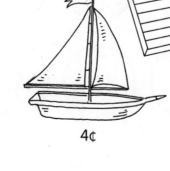

2¢

4¢

_____ ¢ ◯ _____ ¢ = _____ ¢

15 Count the money.
Write the amount.

_____¢

16 Model with pennies.

You have 10¢.

You use 2¢ to buy a pencil.

Write a number sentence.

_____¢ – _____¢ = _____¢

GO ON

17 Write the missing numbers on the calendar.
Tell how you know what to write.

March

Sunday	Monday	Tuesday	Wednesday	Thursday	Friday	Saturday
1	2	3	4		6	7
	9	10	11	12		14
15	16	17		19	20	
22	23	24	25		27	28
29		31				

....

18 Tell how these clocks are alike and different.

Show 6 o'clock on these clocks.

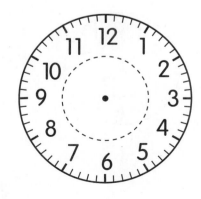

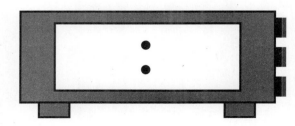

19 Draw two things you like to do.
Circle which takes longer.

···

20 The baby took a nap at 2 o'clock.
He woke up at 4 o'clock.
For how many hours did he sleep?

_____ hours

STOP

Choose the correct answer.

1 About how many 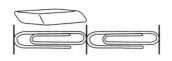 long?

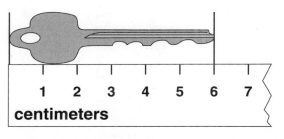

Ⓐ about 1

Ⓒ about 3

Ⓑ about 2

Ⓓ about 4

2 How many inches long?

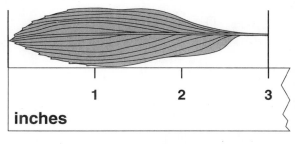

Ⓕ 1 inch   Ⓗ 3 inches
Ⓖ 2 inches Ⓙ 4 inches

3 How many centimeters long?

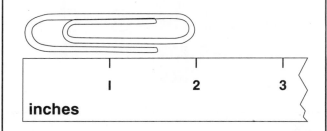

Ⓐ 3 centimeters
Ⓑ 4 centimeters
Ⓒ 5 centimeters
Ⓓ 6 centimeters

4 How many inches long?

Ⓕ 1 inch
Ⓖ 2 inches
Ⓗ 3 inches
Ⓙ 4 inches

Use the pictures to answer questions 5 and 6.

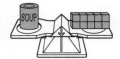  

5 Which is the lightest?

Ⓐ   Ⓑ   Ⓒ

6 Which is the heaviest?

Ⓕ   Ⓖ   Ⓗ

© Harcourt

7 What would you use to measure the length of this?

 A   **B**

8 What would you use to measure the weight of this?

 F   **G**

9 Which figure shows one-half?

 **A**    **C**

B   **D**

10 Which figure shows one-fourth?

F   **H**

G   **J**

11 Which picture shows $\frac{1}{4}$ of the strawberries colored?

A

B

C

D

12 Which picture shows 1 of the candles lit?

F

G

H

J

 GO ON

13. How long is a bus?
What is the best object to use to find out?
Tell why.

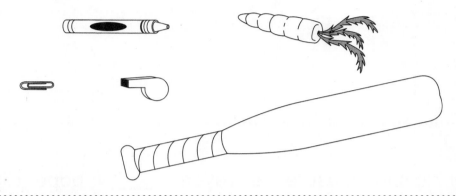

14. Find two objects to compare. Draw them.

Which is longer? How do you know?

15. Draw pictures. Compare.
Tell how you know.

These are longer than my arm.	These are shorter than my arm.

GO ON

16 Draw 2 things you can measure with a ruler.
Tell how you can measure each one.

....

17 Use paper clips to measure the crayon. ____ paper clips
Then use a centimeter ruler. ____ centimeters
Are the measurements the same or different?
Why?

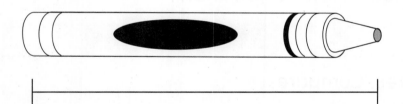

....

18 Which is heavier, the box or the airplane? _____
How do you know?

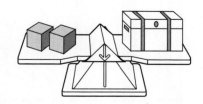 

GO ON

© Harcourt

19 Which container holds more?

Which container holds less?

How do you know?

20 Draw a circle around each shape that shows fourths.

Tell why the shapes you circled show fourths.

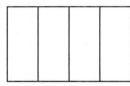

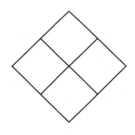
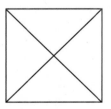

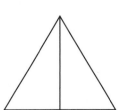

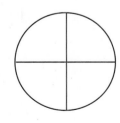

© Harcourt

STOP

Choose the correct answer.

1 How are the dogs sorted?

Ⓐ big–little
Ⓑ black–white
Ⓒ round–square
Ⓓ NOT HERE

2 How many dogs are white?

	Tally Marks	Total
black	II	2
white	IIII	4

Ⓕ 1   Ⓗ 2
Ⓖ 3   Ⓙ NOT HERE

Use the tally table and the graph to answer questions 3 to 6.

	Favorite Toys	Total
truck	III	3
doll	I	1
drum	IIII	
ball	II	2

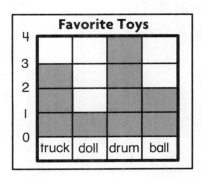

3 Which number is missing from the tally table?

Ⓐ 2   Ⓒ 4
Ⓑ 3   Ⓓ NOT HERE

4 How many children like dolls the best?

Ⓕ 1 child   Ⓗ 6 children
Ⓖ 4 children   Ⓙ NOT HERE

5 Which toy do children like the best?

Ⓐ truck   Ⓒ drum
Ⓑ doll   Ⓓ ball

6 How many more children like drums than dolls?

Ⓕ 1 child   Ⓗ 3 children
Ⓖ 2 children   Ⓙ NOT HERE

GO ON

Name _____

Use the graph for questions 7 and 8.

Balls					Total
baseball	⚾	⚾	⚾		3
football	🏈				1
soccer ball	⚽	⚽	⚽	⚽	4

7 How many footballs are there?

- Ⓐ 1 football
- Ⓑ 2 footballs
- Ⓒ 3 footballs
- Ⓓ 4 footballs

8 How many balls in all?

- Ⓕ 5 balls
- Ⓖ 6 balls
- Ⓗ 7 balls
- Ⓙ 8 balls

Use the graph for questions 9 to 12.

Our Pets		Total
dog	🐕🐕🐕🐕🐕🐕	6
cat	🐈🐈🐈🐈	4
fish	🐟🐟🐟	3

9 How many children have fish?

- Ⓐ 2 children
- Ⓒ 4 children
- Ⓑ 3 children
- Ⓓ 5 children

10 How many more children have dogs than cats?

- Ⓕ 1 child
- Ⓗ 3 children
- Ⓖ 2 children
- Ⓙ 4 children

11 How many more children have dogs than fish?

- Ⓐ 1 child
- Ⓒ 3 children
- Ⓑ 2 children
- Ⓓ NOT HERE

12 How many pets do the children have in all?

- Ⓕ 10 pets
- Ⓗ 12 pets
- Ⓖ 11 pets
- Ⓙ 13 pets

13 Sort the shapes.

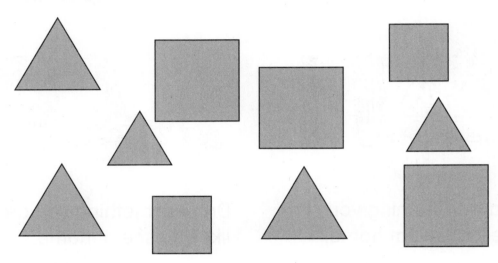

Make a table.

Shapes	Tally Marks	Total

14 Use the graph to answer the question.

Which sport do most children like best?

_____

Our Favorite Sports				
soccer	⚽	⚽		
basketball	🏀	🏀	🏀	
baseball	⚾	⚾	⚾	⚾

© Harcourt

GO ON

15 Circle which you are more likely to see.

Draw something you are likely to see at home.

Draw something you are not likely to see at home.

....

16 Georgine spun this pointer.

This chart shows the outcome of 10 spins.

Pointer Spins	
dark	IIII
light	HHT I

What do you think will happen if Georgine spins the pointer 20 times? _____

_____

GO ON

17 This pointer can stop on 1, 2, or 3.

Which number is the pointer most likely to stop on?

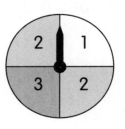

_____

....

18 Get some coins.

Sort them.

Make a graph.

Talk about the graph.

Coins								
pennies								
nickels								
dimes								

GO ON

19 What does the graph show?

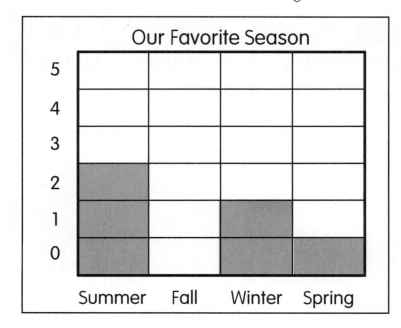

Our Favorite Season

20 Ms. Garcia's class did a survey of their favorite juices. Here are the results.

Our Favorite Juices	
orange	||||
grape	⊦⊦⊦ |
apple	⊦⊦⊦ ⊦⊦⊦

Use the tallies to make a bar graph.

Our Favorite Juices

orange										
grape										
apple										
	1	2	3	4	5	6	7	8	9	10

STOP

Name _____

Choose the correct answer.

1

$4 + 4 = 8$

$4 + 3 = $ _____

(A) 5   (C) 7
(B) 6   (D) 8

2

$$\begin{array}{r} 9 \\ + 9 \\ \hline 18 \end{array} \qquad \begin{array}{r} 9 \\ + 8 \\ \hline \end{array}$$

(F) 16   (H) 18
(G) 17   (J) 19

3

$7 + 8 = $ _____

(A) 12   (C) 14
(B) 13   (D) NOT HERE

4

$6 + 7 = $ _____

(F) 13   (H) 15
(G) 14   (J) NOT HERE

5 Jenna had some hats. Joe gave her 3 more. Now she has 6.

How many hats did she have to start?

(A) 2 caps   (C) 4 caps
(B) 3 caps   (D) 5 caps

6

$5 + 5 = $ _____

$10 - 5 = 5$

(F) 8   (H) 10
(G) 9   (J) 12

GO ON

7 Make a 10. Then add.

$$\begin{array}{r} 8 \\ + 6 \\ \hline \end{array}$$

(A) 11   (C) 13
(B) 12   (D) 14

8

$$\begin{array}{r} 9 \\ + 6 \\ \hline \end{array}$$

(F) 14   (H) 16
(G) 15   (J) NOT HERE

9

$$\begin{array}{r} 4 \\ 4 \\ + 7 \\ \hline \end{array}$$

(A) 13   (C) 15
(B) 14   (D) 16

10

$$\begin{array}{r} 7 \\ 3 \\ + 2 \\ \hline \end{array}$$

(F) 12   (H) 14
(G) 13   (J) 15

11

$$\begin{array}{r} 8 \\ + 7 \\ \hline 15 \end{array} \qquad \begin{array}{r} 15 \\ - 7 \\ \hline \end{array}$$

(A) 5   (C) 7
(B) 6   (D) 8

12

$$\begin{array}{r} 9 \\ + 4 \\ \hline 13 \end{array} \qquad \begin{array}{r} 13 \\ - 4 \\ \hline \end{array}$$

(F) 6   (H) 8
(G) 7   (J) 9

GO ON

13 Read the story. Then write a number sentence to solve.

There are 7 red apples and 6 yellow apples in the bowl.
How many apples are there in all?

_____ + _____ = _____

....

14 Draw ◯ to show 5 + 5.

Write the sum. 5 + 5 = _____

Draw ◯ to show 5 + 4.

Write the addition sentence. _____ + _____ = _____

GO ON

15 Write a number sentence.

Solve the problem.

Sam has 14 airplanes.

Sue has 7 airplanes.

How many more airplanes does Sam have than Sue?

_____ − _____ = _____

16 Draw counters in the ten-frames.

Show how you find the sum.

$$\begin{array}{r} 7 \\ + 9 \\ \hline \end{array}$$

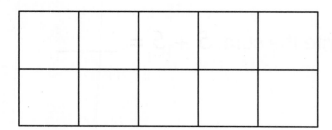

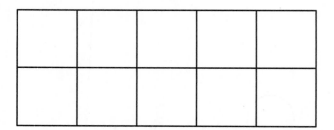

17 Solve the problem.

Six children are in the lunch line.

Two children get out of the line.

Then two new children get in the line.

How many children are in the lunch line now? _____ children

GO ON

18 Write a number sentence. Solve.

Pablo gave Kristen 4 crayons.

Now Kristen has 12 crayons.

How many crayons did she have to start?

_____ + _____ = _____

....

19 What is the missing addend?

$5 + \boxed{} = 11$

Draw cubes to show.

....

20 What is the missing addend?

$9 + \boxed{} = 16$

Draw a picture to show.

STOP

Name _____

Choose the correct answer.

1 How many counters?

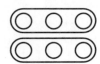

Ⓐ 3 counters Ⓒ 6 counters
Ⓑ 5 counters Ⓓ 8 counters

2 How many in each group?

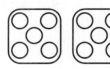

Ⓕ 4 counters Ⓗ 6 counters
Ⓖ 5 counters Ⓙ 7 counters

3 How many in each group?

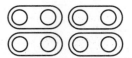

Ⓐ 2 counters Ⓒ 6 counters
Ⓑ 4 counters Ⓓ 8 counters

4 How many groups?

Ⓕ 2 groups Ⓗ 4 groups
Ⓖ 3 groups Ⓙ 5 groups

5 There are 3 groups.
Each group has 3
counters.

How many counters are
there in all?

Ⓐ 3 counters Ⓒ 8 counters
Ⓑ 6 counters Ⓓ 9 counters

6 There are 2 cars.
Each has 4 people in it.

How many people are
there in all?

Ⓕ 2 people
Ⓖ 4 people
Ⓗ 6 people
Ⓙ 8 people

GO ON

Name _____

7 Add.

tens	ones

$$
\begin{array}{r}
20 \\
+\ 10 \\
\hline
\end{array}
$$

Ⓐ 3   Ⓒ 30
Ⓑ 20   Ⓓ 31

8 Add.

tens	ones

$$
\begin{array}{r}
5\ \ 5 \\
+\ 2\ \ 1 \\
\hline
\end{array}
$$

Ⓕ 6   Ⓗ 86
Ⓖ 76   Ⓙ NOT HERE

9 Add.

tens	ones

$$
\begin{array}{r}
3\ \ 3 \\
+\ 3\ \ 5 \\
\hline
\end{array}
$$

Ⓐ 14   Ⓒ 68
Ⓑ 67   Ⓓ 86

10 Subtract.

tens	ones

$$
\begin{array}{r}
4\ \ 5 \\
-\ 3\ \ 4 \\
\hline
\end{array}
$$

Ⓕ 11   Ⓗ 19
Ⓖ 12   Ⓙ 79

11 Subtract.

tens	ones

$$
\begin{array}{r}
6\ \ 4 \\
-\ 2\ \ 1 \\
\hline
\end{array}
$$

Ⓐ 3   Ⓒ 35
Ⓑ 33   Ⓓ 43

12 Choose the answer that makes sense.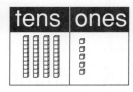

Joe had 49 pennies. He gave 25 pennies to Jill. How many pennies does he have left?

Ⓕ 4   Ⓗ 64
Ⓖ 24   Ⓙ 240

Math Advantage Georgia Test Prep   56   **GO ON** ➡

© Harcourt

13 Draw. Use ◯. Make 2 groups.

Put 5 ◯ in each group.

How many ◯ are there in all? _____

· ·

14 Draw. Use 10 ◯.

Make 5 equal groups.

How many ◯ are in each group? _____

GO ON

Name _____

15 Draw 12 ◯. Put 6 in each group.

How many groups did you make?   _____ groups

....

16 Draw a picture to solve.

There are 15 stars. They are in 5 equal groups.

How many stars are in each group?

_____ stars

....

17 Nat saved 38 pennies last month.

He saved 54 pennies this month.

How many pennies did Nat save in all?

_____ pennies

GO ON ➡

18 Use base-ten blocks and solve.

There are 27 ducks in the pond.

18 swim away.

How many ducks are left?

_____ ducks

....

19 How much money would you need to buy both?

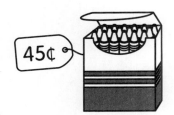

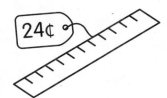

Choose the operation and solve. Write + or –.

◯ 45 ¢
24 ¢

____

....

20 Add or subtract to solve the problem.

You have 75¢.

You buy a fish.

How much money do you have left?

_____ ¢

STOP